YO-BNW-475

Invisible
Hands

A BOOK OF POETRY

HARKI DHILLON

ISBN:0-615-49738-1

ISBN-13:978-0-615-49738-9

LCCN:2011932419

Contents

Thanksgiving

The cold. The dark.

The wind. The stars.

The tent.

The dog. The children.

The food.

Thanksgiving.

The fire.

Struggling with the wind

the flaps on the tent

whipping in the wind

tears

in the cold, in the wind

stars so bright. So near,

once every year

nature purges

all urban concerns

on

Thanksgiving.

Last Night

The golden rays of
the early morning sun
touch her hair.
Her gentle breathing
muffled
by the rumpled sheets
that cover her carelessly,
the painted toe nail
peeking out,
as her foot
dangles off the edge.
I remember her delight,
last night
at retrieving the sprinkled cup cake
from the little brown bag
and wolfing it down
with the chilled champagne
As she looked at me
so directly
so invitingly
last night.

I saw the palm frond fall

I saw the palm frond fall
through the clear blue sky
its graceful descent
cushioned by the
invisible hands
of the gentle breeze.
It hits the asphalt
and rocks into stillness
its final moment
lasts but a second
shattered by the
great, big wheels of the SUV
crushing it into
its final remains,
obliterated by the rushing sedans
and finally, respectfully
encouraged into
the gutter
by the same gentle breeze
that helped to give grace
to a final moment
before eternity.

Love

The parched, caked earth
cracked, in irregular
geometric forms.
parched and dry
looking to the heavens
for relief,
crying a little more
every day.
In this soulless desolation,
seemingly insignificant,
a circle of bricks
covered by corrugated
sheets of iron
held down by
more bricks.
Love passes over
as a gentle breeze
easily lifting the
metal cover
without a noise,
exposing
the dark, sweet water
which

rises to the surface

flowing easily,

restoring

hope and life

to the body and soul.

The Inn

The birth of an idea

the stroking of an ego

the vision

the purpose

the money

the Mission.

Piety in the Chapel

glamour with the gold.

Thoughtlessness

beyond my death.

People left

to shore up crumbling walls

responsibility for history

serving one's pride.

The vision,

bringing the City and People

together

in the future.

I Am

Mind, body and soul
overtaken
by the business of living
little volcanic eruptions
of creativity
deep within
beginning to see the light of day.
Emotional debris
mixed with the soot and ash
of experience,
distracting, but enhancing
the quality of my own perception
of life.
Bread on the table
joy in my heart
music in my soul.
That's what I long for.
Let it not implode
leaving only
ash and soot and debris.

The memories lie buried

The memories lie buried

of

The heady days of confusion

of

Love, lust, longing and loneliness,

of

heat and sweat,

exhaustion and exhilaration

of

The fog and the clarity

of youth,

of

The me and the my

and the mine

of

the loss and the pain and

the agony

of the smile and the swagger

and the hope of

the reluctant rejuvenation.

As, the new world opens.

As the new life begins,

as the memories lie buried,

in the dust of responsibility,

as the memories lie buried

in the treasured vault.

As the memories lie buried

except

for that cerebral lapse

that shows the sunlit

and silent street,

as lovers we walk

footsteps fading

into the present

as memories lie buried

of

those heady days of confusion.

I Imagine

Your dark eyes

haunt me

with their intensity.

Tales of betrayal

in your life

inhabit my thoughts.

The empty shell

of your emotions

confuses me,

because,

I imagine

those eyes closed

by an intensity

of a reverberating

orgasm,

by the intensity

of your uninhibited smile,

by the ferocity

of your

fingers entwined

in mine,

by the soft touch

of your breast

on my arm

as you lean on me,

your head on my shoulder

your life fulfilled.

I Had Imagined

I had imagined
the world
full of laughter
but
people
got in the way.

I had imagined
the world
full of love
but
egos
got in the way.

I had imagined
the world
full of friends
but
race and religion
got in the way.

I've been in the world
a while now.

I try and hang on

to my sanity

with hope

but

life gets in the way.

The Arc of the Sun

The sun rises,

peeks over the horizon.

The baby opens its eyes,

gurgles,

and seeks the engorged breast.

The sun reaches its zenith,

casts the tiniest shadows

of the mightiest structures.

The invincibility of youth

has changed me, I'm

teetering on the edge,

looking at the vulnerability

of coming years.

The sun sinks towards

the horizon,

a golden glow

casting deep and dark shadows.

Darkness comes, taking light

and life away,

one of them, forever.

Total Joint Replacement

I hurt,

I weep,

drowning in

my own tears.

I feel guilt,

not serving my

master well,

they will attack me

with

knife and saw,

burn me, replace me.

They will do it humanely.

I will feel no pain.

It will end

in my sacrifice.

My end will be

for the greater good.

I was active, in pain.

I am no more

but

I can move.

Soulless, I exist.

The colors of the Rainbow

The rain stops suddenly.
The thunder clouds
dark and menacing
have discharged their load
of heavy raindrops,
which splatter
on earth bound objects
with suicidal ferocity.
The foreboding darkness
in daylight
gets pushed away
by
tentative and apologetic
sunlight
in the now oh so clear air.
The rainbow magically appears
in its brilliant colors
and brings an undefined cheeriness.
I look up at the sky
just before I enter the hospital
to the blaring
soul disturbing
sounds of code red

soon followed by

code blue, code green, code orange,

yellow, pink and shades of grey.

Fire, death, distress, abduction,

bombs and the response

all represented

by the brilliant

colors of the rainbow.

My silent Friend

I talk to you
ceaselessly,
you pat me on my back,
you criticize gently.
You encouraged me.
I form a plan,
you nod your acknowledgement.
Who are you,
my silent friend?

Innocence

The cold, slim hand
holds mine,
pulls me to the dance floor.
I have forgotten
the touch of innocence.
Her hand lingers in mine.
It is brief,
this realization,
before
the music disconnects
this sense
of impropriety.

Med-Mal (Frivolous)/ Plaintiff

"You did wrong.

I will hit back.

I will have my revenge.

I will claim damages.

I will ruin you.

I suffered.

I had, oh sorry,

I have pain.

You did wrong."

Case dismissed, next.

The Middle East

Thousands of years
of conflict,
children of the same God
tear at the fabric
of each other's existence.

A deep mistrust
founded in the nebulous shadows
of history,
fueled by the fires of belief.

The external voice
of reason
does not dent
the armored resolve
of
the righteous.

Passion of penance,
indication of guilt,
the destruction
of the house
that Jack built.

Remorse, regret and reaffirmation

stop the bleeding

attempt to heal

the conscience of a people

already, probably,

irrevocably,

destroyed.

ICU

The rhythmic puffing
sounds of hope,
merged with despair,
mingled with a prayer,
interwoven
with the sighs of unanswered questions.

The curtain, apologetically,
is half drawn,
a boundary
as definite
as a two foot
thick wall.

The fluorescent lights
and voices outside,
a stark contrast
to the silence and semi-darkness within
the room
and in my soul.

Another presence,
an encouraging smile,

deft hands
manipulate, assess
and record
the lingering, struggling,
dormant
signs of life.

This is just the
tenth day,
a lifetime, already,
yet
hope lives
because
it is the tenth day.

I wake up on
the eleventh day,
dreading the visit
but
eager to sit in my
chair, in the left
hand corner at the
foot of the bed.

I arrive,
bathed and dressed
and spruced up
for hours of

prayer and negotiation.
My eyes open wide,
as open eyes look back
at me.
I see you.

Treachery

The sanctity
of solitude
and space,
violated
by a mindless intrusion.
No defense.
Troy relived.
Treachery
from within.

The Misty Veil

The misty veil of
the mountain
lifted
by
the fawning, cajoling, caressing
attention of the wind,
ably assisted
by the
strengthening rays of
gleaming sunlight.
The snow capped peak
arching its phallic mass
towards
the teasing, blue sky,
retreating just as quickly
behind
the misty veil,
mildly ashamed
of flaunting
its Majesty.

Healing glue

Healing glue
for broken bones,
for torn muscles.
Blood on the asphalt
shining on broken glass.
Blood replaced.
Metal and stitches
put me together,
physically.
Mind messed up
afraid, anxious, unsure.
Pen to paper,
thoughts flowing,
irrelevant, scattered, sobbing.
Healing glue
finally
saved my soul,
my mind.

Eagle Eyes

The fine restaurant,
table cloths and
ultra clean glass,
soft, constant recognizable
decibels of conversation.
A snooty waiter and
a wine list as long as the
towel on his forearm.
Dim lights,
a necessity of fine dining,
as necessary as a
vintage bottle of wine.
The prices are matched
by the number of zeroes
with a dot somewhere in between,
hidden well to confuse the price.
I borrow my friend's glasses.
It all becomes clear.
I was going to pay too much.
It was a defining moment.
Eagle eyes 20/20
had shown the first sign of age.
A small jolt

followed

by a sense of loss,

years later reinforced

by a little more blurring

on the menu and the wine list.

This time the steak

did not lose its appeal.

The wine was aged well.

I was trying to

do the same.

Insignificance

The depth of the cosmos,

the infinity of space,

the infinitesimal scale of us

related to the Universe.

Yet, we exist,

unfazed

by the size of our imagination

and ego

and the depths of our emotion,

the power of our love

and our hate,

the foundations of

our existence,

unstable

in the insecurity of

our psyche,

held together

with the promise of

Divine love.

The freedom from barriers

that encompass deeply

held feelings

coming from a focus of

complete trust
without fear of rejection
and ridicule.
The ability to say
the Name
in silence, in one's heart
or
shouted with abandon
to the millions.
What else could fulfill this need,
except the concept and belief
in a Supreme Being?
What else could invoke
this commitment
while making one better
in one's soul
for a reward in the after life
that compensates
for the fear
of one's demise.

Disquiet

The breathing sounds of
the house,
an anti-thesis to the living
disquiet within
that will awaken shortly.
Till then
a distant calm
stimulated
by the snowcapped mountains
receding
by each wave of
irrational thought.

Hands

Hands
roam in the Vatican.
Silence, broken
by whispered echoes.
I stand next to a bronze statue
and see the mark of the centuries.
Pious touch has
eroded metal.
Is this the power of belief
or just
mechanics.

Twenty thousand miles away
I see the hand of the Guru
from centuries ago,
imprinted in stone,
submerged in
swirling turquoise water.
A chill envelops me
briefly
replaced
then by the gentle warmth
of being alive.

In the Desert

The air-conditioned comfort,
the powerful engine of this
big mechanical beast,
the laughter and high spirits
roll over the rocks and sand
and the dry river bed,
in the desert.

The engine sputters,
the beast falters.
Silence descends
within.
The vastness extends
in all directions.
Very little water.
Stupidity
in the desert.

The Desert Flower

I am parched.

Let it rain,

but

not too much.

I want to flower and bloom,

not die.

ANGST

My feet touch the fire
in an agony of awakening.
My feet are held there
in a demoralizing spiral.
The soul rises in a lazy swirl
from scorched flesh.
The silent scream
drowns the crescendo
of spasmodic muscles
in a rictus of frustration.
I ache for the balm
of a soothing hand
placed between
my shoulder blades.
A whispering calm
releases me from
my angst –
temporarily – until
the next time
my path is covered
with simmering flames
of burning coal.

A Cool Dessert

The V10 growls under me,
the seat holds me in
a protective embrace
as it noses its way
aggressively
near the rear end of
a disgusting shade of
an unmentionable color on
four wheels, which
leaps ahead to demonstrate
its coquettish, nimble
getaway technique.
I sneer inwardly with
an outward swagger
and park.
The woman crosses my path
as I get out.
She's dressed well and showing
her curves.
She gestures to her friend
with her arm raised
and I look up her short sleeve
to the freshly shaven axilla.

She would be a cool dessert

to a hot sultry afternoon

or

a warm sweet soufflé'

on a winter evening.

Silver hair

Silver hair, glasses,
an empty smile, body robust.
Yet,
she shuffles in
holding her daughter's hand.
She sits down, looking at the floor
as if it may interest her.
I come in, say 'hello',
having met her a few times.
'Who are you?' she asks me.
Maybe my scrubs
alter my appearance.
"He's John's doctor, mum".
She looks at her husband
of fifty years,
she touches his silver hair,
as he lies on the gurney.
'I like him', she says, smiling.
John grins proudly and
gratefully;
"She does remember me', he says,
as we wheel him into surgery.

A maelstrom of emotions

Mists ascend and envelop.
Vista disappears,
ghostly shadows of trees remain
and leave a deepened
 sense of confusion
enhanced by the repetitive call
of a black partridge
echoed by its mate,
hidden in the green cover
of the mountainside.
Flashes reflected off
the swirling mist,
vacationers recording
transient, familial gatherings
while contemplating the infirmity of their elders
and their own inheritance
lurking in the future,
doubting the integrity
of their own blood.
Corrugated iron roofs
over walls of peeling paint
cry out the past
of a Kingdom

of subjugated natives
by a foreign force
with tunics of red.

Involution of time,
the soul curling into
a foetal position
exposed, shivering, vulnerable,
having lost the warmth
of layers of protective fluid.

Shake off the shackles of
regressive inertia
and head back to
that far away land,
now home.

A Sleepless Night

Darkness,

lights unblinking,

numbers changing,

thoughts random,

flitting.

No solutions.

Random thoughts,

not insomnia.

Past and present,

merging images,

connected only by time

and

the thread of the same life.

Unblinking lights,

a focus

of friendly encouragement,

accusatory

for this unwanted attention.

Shadows of memories

reflected on the walls

playing their own stories,

theatrical.

The pulse of the

material world

monitored

by unblinking lights

and changing numbers

of the clock

racing towards dawn.

The light of day

pushing deep and away

images

that meant something.

No solutions.

Incandescence of day

obliterating

all

but the presence

of

current, relevant thought.

A Human Life

A brilliant flash
of light
reflected off
a grain of sand.
A zillion stars
a trillion miles
a billion years,
the Universe.
A human life,
just a brilliant flash
reflected off
a grain of sand.

The Beat

The shoulders that carried the man

in joyful abandon

to the pulsating beat of celebration,

then,

bore the weight of death

to the heavy beat

of remaining hearts.

Farewell

I push deep inside you
overcome
with a sensation
that can only be love.
Tears flow freely
in unashamed ecstasy
compounded by its transience.
I remember the day
you came into my arms.
You swooned
with the intensity
of whatever
you were feeling.
I remember the day
you wrote from
across the oceans
and wished me well.
I don't even know
where you are today.

Surgery

Hands move

in controlled ecstasy,

immersed in

nature's beauty gone wrong.

The depths are exposed

illuminated by

artificial light

and the wisdom of years.

The dance of the fingers

choreographed by experience,

synchronous

with the aim

of initiating

a cure

of a malady

inflicting

this unfortunate body.

The Immigrant

Thoughts, emotions
flash across the oceans
and giant landmasses,
erupting, welling, simmering
in spite of
present preoccupations.

The Maze

Guide me through
this maze
my friend.
I tire of my wandering.
I need your hand.
I admit
your strength
is my weakness.
Maybe I can help
you someday.
I hope.

The Fire

The fire burns with
a frivolous intensity
happy with its fuel.
It means no harm
as it accidentally burns
me
when I get too close.
I do not curse
anything but
my own stupidity.

Garden of Doubt

I wander the pre-ordained path,

surrounded

by beauty and smells

of flowers in bloom

yet,

I feel

I am in

the Garden of Doubt.

You crossed the line

You crossed the line,
you took sides,
you left
an unsightly gash in
the emotional wall
of dependent love.

Waves of sadness
drip through the rent
hoping
the well never runs dry.

Hoping,
a hint of remorse
from you
will reach across
like balm
to seal the wound

Turquoise and Green

Mountain

arrogant

forest

slopes

silence

broken by

the gentle sound of flowing water

in the meandering

streams of

turquoise and green.

The eye skips upstream

over the tiny waves

to it's unseen origins

in the mighty glacier,

the power of its frozen contents

shaping

the curves of submission

in the proud, rugged and

near vertical projections

of earth and rock.

All of it
still
resulting in the
meandering streams of
turquoise and green.

Snow

The leaves of the conifer
like fingers entwined
hold
the gently falling snow.
The thaw
exposed this masquerade
as the snow
changes to water
and leaves its
lingering embrace,
not ungrateful.
I reach out
and pick up
what remains,
still entangled,
the brilliant white snow
in it's bouncy green bed.
I disturb nature
at it's most compatible
for my curiosity
to feel the exquisite sensation
of purity

melting in my mouth.
The branch springs up
releasing a projectile of snow,
a frivolous and friendly gesture
or an attempt
to spit in my eye.

Loneliness

The blowing wind
rustles my mind,
already agitated.

The blowing wind
calms my mind,
receptive
to its indifference
to all things human.

The leaves in the trees
rustle continuously
in the daylight
in a repetitive
ululation,
bringing a smile to my lips.

It is night.
The leaves rustle,
now with menace,
in continuous spasms
in the speckled moonlight.

Ghosts move
uninhibited
nourished by their thoughts
and fears.
They touch my goosebumps,
stimulate the erector pilorum.
My fingers flex against
the arms of
the hundred year old
rocking chair.
The tendons strain
responding to their
cerebral master.

Pre-dawn is disturbed
by the morning alarm.
A cheery voice
declares a sig alert.

I prepare for the day
by stepping in the shower
 letting the hot water
ease the pain
of my loneliness.

Worlds Apart

Diets changed,
dal and roti,
hands and fingers
to
Shepherd's Pie and Dijon,
knife and fork.
Tea remained.
Wine on table,
red and white cloth,
hospital dosas gone,
replaced with
minestrone, peas
and mushroom.

Worlds Apart part II

Crowded OPDs,

patients

and all their attendants

in rags and shrouds

standardizing silhouettes.

Sounds, clamoring voices

seeking much wanted

attention. So in your face!

One plane journey

turned everything

on its head.

Spotless office,

sole occupancy,

patient escorted by nurse

on color coded lines

to X-ray or lab.

Polite conversation,

sparkling floors

a new and different world.

Life

Life,
a pulsating force
ensures all manner
of subterfuge
to succeed.
It is cloaked in a body
that shelters the mind
which schemes and manipulates
with the tools
of love and kindness,
of hate and lies.
Sometimes
remorse and regret
get in the way.

The Chasm

I stood at the edge

to take flight,

to soar,

to see the blue of the sky

not the darkness of despair.

Why were you so cruel?

Where did the love go?

The song in my heart

was yours to hear

but

the chasm

was too wide,

the echoes

too

disconcerting.

Time

Time is alive,
a continuum.
The past merges
into the present
and
stretches into
the unknown.
We live occasionally
without trauma
and disease,
a good innings.
Yet
it is a mere flash.
We rejoice
in that extra year
that good genes
let us breathe, see,
smell and hear
and
share that moment
with loved ones.

My Daughter

I have looked upon
and adored this face
for all these years.
The addition of her life,
her energy, her laugh,
her silences to mine
has forever
completed the purpose
of my existence.
Every moment of togetherness
shared
is a ray of sunshine
to a starving soul.
It is the quantum of strength
that builds the core,
to overcome
most of what
life throws at me.

Purple Light

Purple light
reflecting off mountainous might.
Sunset snow
taking its final bow.
Sunset dread and
dark thoughts to bed.
Chilled bones
in shivering tones.
You come under the duvet
and curl around my fetal form.
Your dry lips touch my neck
not wanting anything
but emotional warmth.
Churning minds and beating hearts come together
wanting nothing
but a moment of calm.
A deep longing emerges
making the throat dry
and toes curl
in a paradox of pain and pleasure.
Night moves in,
into the comfort
of broken solitude.

The involuntary shiver
acknowledging the presence
of my mate.

The Gentle Waltz

The woman tripped along
her heart full of song,
a lazy smile on her lips
and a graceful
wiggle to her hips.

Golden light bathed
the countryside,
vanishing dew drops
glittered before they died.
She saw the welcoming meadow with the white wooden gate,
she hurried through it,
a trifle late.

He lay amongst the flowers
waiting for her,
blue eyes drinking blue sky,
fingers flitting over the petals,
fingers stroking the stems.

He sensed her presence
and rose
like life itself

from Mother earth.

She ran into the arms

of her beau,

crushed in his embrace,

declarations of love

coming at a fevered pace,

her body arching to his,

fingertips wandering

to undo her lace.

Spent,

they drifted above

in a gentle waltz,

their bodies entwined

in a cocoon of love.

Index